MEN
ARE
BASTARDS

ALL MEN ARE BASTARDS

Myra Venge

aided not inconsiderably by
Stephen Blake and Andrew John

Michael O'Mara Humour

First published in Great Britain in 2002 by
Michael O'Mara Books Limited
9 Lion Yard
Tremadoc Road
London SW4 7NQ

Copyright © Michael O'Mara Books Ltd 2002

The material in this compilation first appeared in
101 Unpleasant Things About Men and *The Little Book of
Stupid Men* © Michael O'Mara Books Ltd. Additional
material (pages 180-194) taken from *Quotes from Women on
Top* by Jasmine Birtles
© 1996 Michael O'Mara Books Ltd.

A CIP catalogue record for this book is available from
the British Library

ISBN 1-85479-387-X

1 3 5 7 9 10 8 6 4 2

Designed and typeset by Design 23

Printed and bound by Bookmarque Limited, UK

Male, *n*: a member of the unconsidered, or negligible sex. The male of the human race is commonly known to the female as Mere Man. The genus has two varieties: good providers and bad providers.

AMBROSE BIERCE,
The Devil's Dictionary

INTRODUCTION

I've had it *right up to here* with men.
Men are layabouts and louts,
chauvinists, misogynists, bigamists,
polygamists; they're blockheads, nitwits,
halfwits and dolts, dunces, dunderheads
and fools; men are corrupt, iniquitous,
depraved and villainous; they're vicious,
malicious, malevolent and downright
demonic. Need I go on? In short, all men
are bastards!

I do, of course, excuse the cute lads who
helped me compile this tribute to all
that's unpleasant, disagreeable, wicked
and corrupt, repugnant and repellent,
loathsome, sickening, disgusting, base
and *bad* about men. Thanks, guys!

THEY'RE SOOOO INFURIATING!

My purpose here is to make you see men for what they are. If you're a man, tough titties. Read on: you may learn something. Here are some of my pet hates ...

Men think farting is funny.

•

They call you 'babe'.

•

Not one man in any beer commercial has a beer belly. Could this be because all the adverts are made by men?

•

It's petrol-station flowers after only one year of marriage.

•

Men disappear into the bathroom for hours with the newspapers.

•

They always try to solve your problems instead of just being sympathetic about them.

•

They pick their noses and wipe it under the sofa, or on the headboard.

They adjust themselves very publicly with no shame whatsoever.

•

They think you might actually enjoy a sweaty hug.

•

They leave 'used tissues' under the bed.

•

It's never 'please, could you – ?'; it's only ever 'When are *we* [meaning you] going to – ?'

•

They throw away your dried flowers – 'Well, they were dead, weren't they?'

•

They can't tell when their trainers stink.

•

They never look for their passports until an hour before take-off.

•

They're horrid to your cat.

•

They leave their Christmas shopping till Christmas Eve so they end up grabbing the nearest most unsuitable thing.

They buy you size-8 black, prickly lacy underwear.

•

They perm their hair and wear nylon track suits and think they're being *soooo* cool.

•

They channel-surf so much you forget what you're supposed to be watching.

•

They put their guts before their hearts (literally).

•

They comb their hair over their bald patches.

•

They take great pleasure in passing their mates pictures of tits and general porn (what else is e-mail for?), and having a good laugh over them.

•

They're always bragging about their sexual performance!

AND NOW, A WORD ON TOENAILS...

Unlike women, men are incapable of clipping their toenails in a discreet fashion. Instead, they have to clip them to maximum annoying effect, so that razor-sharp shards go volleying and ricocheting in all directions, embed themselves in the upholstery and the carpet, land in your cuppa etc, and you end up picking them up from things or out of things for days, nay weeks, to come.

Either that or they leave a little pile of clippings here and there, like territorial markings, in wholly inappropriate places, like the mantelpiece, the arm of a chair or the coffee table.

WHEN WILL THEY EVER LEARN?

Old habits die hard

'Boys pride themselves on their drab clothing, their droopy socks, their smeared and inky skin: dirt, for them, is almost as good as wounds. They work at acting like boys. They call each other by their last names, draw attention to any extra departures from cleanliness ... There always seem to be more of them in a room than there actually are.'

MARGARET ATWOOD, writer

'A man speaks only when driven to speech by something outside himself – like, for instance, he can't find any clean socks.'

JEAN KERR, playwright

•

What do a clitoris, an anniversary, and a toilet have in common?

Men always miss them.

OK, it's a joke, but it's all too true, sadly...

AFFECTIONATE MEN

Do you know what it means to come home to a man who'll give you a little love, a little affection, a little tenderness?

It means you're in the wrong house.

MEN ALWAYS KNOW BEST

Isn't it annoying how men always refuse to ask directions – both while travelling and in bed? This is, of course, because they know everything, and who are we to contradict them?

'Men know everything – all of them – all the time – no matter how stupid or inexperienced or arrogant or ignorant they are.'

ANDREA DWORKIN, feminist writer

'Men are unable to admit that they are wrong, no matter how lightweight the issue.'

SONYA FRIEDMAN, writer

'Men will *not* change unless they have to.'

DORA RUSSELL,
social activist and writer

'The only thing that consoles man for the stupid things he does is the praise he always gives himself for doing them.'

OSCAR WILDE,
playwright, poet and wit

THEY'RE SUCH ANIMALS!

It just makes you want to give it all up and get a pet. However, here's a warning for those women who have canine preferences ...

How Dogs And Men Are The Same

Both take up too much space on the bed.

•

Both have irrational fears about vacuum cleaning.

•

Both are threatened by their own kind.

•

Both like to chew wood.

•

Both mark their territory.

•

Both are bad at asking you questions.

Neither tells you what's bothering them.
Both tend to smell riper with age.

•

The smaller ones tend to be more nervous.

•

Neither does any dishes.

•

Neither of them notices when you get your hair cut.

•

Both like dominance games.

•

Both are suspicious of the postman.

•

Neither knows how to talk on the telephone.

•

Neither understands what you see in cats.

MALE CHAUVINIST PIGS AND OTHER ANIMALS

Oink oink oink!

'To each masquerading male the female is a mirror in which he beholds himself.'
        KATE MILLETT, feminist writer

'Have you ever wondered why there are so many men in the "right-to-life" movement and so few in child care?'
        LETTY COTTIN POGREBIN,
                feminist writer

'A man is entitled to issue blunt orders, contradict people flatly, instruct or command or forbid outright, without apology or circumlocution.'
        DOROTHY DINNERSTEIN, feminist

'... no one is more arrogant toward women, more aggressive or scornful, than the man who is anxious about his virility.'

SIMONE DE BEAUVOIR, novelist

'Show me a woman who doesn't feel guilty and I'll show you a man.'

ERICA JONG, writer and poet

LIES, DAMNED LIES
AND MEN

'Sigh no more, ladies,
sigh no more,
Men were deceivers ever.'

WILLIAM SHAKESPEARE,
Much Ado About Nothing

PROFESSIONAL LIES ONLY MEN CAN TELL

Ooh! Suits you, sir!

May I help you?

I'll be right with you.

I'll order it for you.

Two days.

Don't worry, it'll shrink.

It's so *you.*

That *is* your size.

Don't worry, it'll stretch.

I'll ring you when it's in.

That really suits you.

Money well spent.

I've got the same one at home.

A perfect fit.

Of course.

It'll never give you any trouble.

You never bought that here.

As it's you …

Our most popular model.

I'm trying to help you.

I can explain.

I'm having it sent over
from our other shop.

It's never been used.

We're out of stock.

I'm new here.

Leave your name and number ...

We'll replace it free of charge.

No one else has complained.

It was lost in transit.

One careful owner.

Of course I'm sure.

I can't imagine how
that happened.

DIY LIES

I know what I'm doing.

You're going to thank me for this.

It's nothing.

I've nearly finished.

This won't take long.

This is all your fault.

This is saving us a fortune.

I just have to make one little adjustment.

According to the news in March 2001, there are 99,000 injuries every year in DIY-related activities – 40,000 involving ladders. Now you wouldn't catch any self-respecting woman up a ladder when there are gullible men around to do things for us ...

I WOULD GET MORE INVOLVED WITH THE KIDS, BUT ...

I can't.

My dad never did that.

They *are* more important than my job, but...

Any night but tonight.

Of course I don't mind changing nappies.

Of course I want to go to the school concert, but...

I would if I could.

Of course, I wouldn't miss it for the world, but...

Next time.

MEN'S LIES TO THEIR OFFSPRING

'We'll stop for lunch just around the next corner…' Yeah, right Dad!

Father knows best.

Of course I'll understand.

Fighting never settled anything.

It's got nothing to do with me. You'll have to ask your mother.

We'll settle this fairly.

I'm busy right now.

Of course I wouldn't have preferred a son.

Of course I approve, but you know what your mother's like.

I'll tell you when you're old enough to understand.

It's not a question of money.

It isn't me I'm worried about.
It's your mother.

There's nothing to worry about.

The stork.

I never said any such thing.

My door is always open.

Yes, I'm listening to you.

You won't be punished if you tell me the
truth.

I'm not avoiding anything.

I hear exactly what you're saying.

This'll hurt me more than it hurts you.

This will break your mother's heart.

I did it for you.

MEN'S ATTITUDE TOWARDS KIDS

'Only men could be responsible for the belief that a boy child is to be preferred to a girl child.'

MARGARET FULLER, feminist writer

'Men do not want to have to take care of children. Rule them, yes. Play with them, yes. Take credit for their achievements, certainly. But not care for their bottles, diapers, mess, spills, tears, tantrums, laundry, lunches, nightmares and the million daily details of childhood.'

LETTY COTTIN POGREBIN, feminist writer

MEN ARE JUST BIG KIDS

Frogs and snails and puppy dogs'
tails ...

'Boys will be boys, and so will a lot of
middle-aged men.'
> KIN HUBBARD (Frank McKinney
> Hubbard), humorist

'A man's worst difficulties begin when
he is able to do as he likes.'
> T. H. HUXLEY, scientist

SIMPLY TERRIBLE THINGS MEN SAY ABOUT US WOMEN

Men can be plain jealous of our superiority and the fact that we can get away with things they can't – or think they can't. Among the things they say about us are ...

We got off the *Titanic* first.

We can scare male bosses with mysterious gynaecological-disorder excuses.

We get to flirt with systems-support men who always return our calls, and are nice to us when we blow up our computers.

We can absently hum tunes from musicals without anyone wondering about our sexuality.

When we buy a vibrator we think it's glamorous. When men buy a blow-up doll we tell them it's pathetic.

We don't have to get our strength up between sessions ... and it's much easier for us to get 'some' in the first place.

We never ejaculate prematurely.

We can get off with teenagers without being called dirty old perverts.

Our boyfriends' clothes make us look elfin and gorgeous – guys look like complete idiots in ours.

We can be groupies. Male groupies are stalkers.

We can cry and get off speeding fines.

We live longer, so we can be cantankerous old biddies wearing inappropriate clothes and shouting at strangers.

Men die earlier so we get to cash in on the life insurance.

Taxis stop for us.

MEN NEVER LISTEN

Just a thought, if a man speaks in the forest and there is no woman there to hear him, is he still wrong?

'As for those who say, "Yes, dear, whatever you say, dear," while doing exactly as they please – they are the worst there is.'

MERLE SHAIN, writer

'Men often wonder what it is they have done wrong.'

ANNA FORD, journalist and
television newsreader

'Men readily interrupt the speech of women, and women allow the interruption.'

SUSAN BROWNMILLER,
feminist writer

OOH YOU LYING GIT!

This has got to be one of the biggest male lies of all time

Actually, I'm a feminist myself.

LIES MEN MAKE TO WOMEN IN GENERAL

You know, those all-purpose lies for every occasion. They all use them!

Men have more logical minds.

You made me do it.

I can't cook.

You asked for it.

Men never gossip.

It's different for a man.

It's your own fault.

I've never hit a woman before.

Women have a natural affinity with dirty nappies that men don't have.

Male superiority.

Hormones.

I'm not just saying this
because I'm drunk.

I don't know how.

A man's gotta do what a
man's gotta do.

SEX LIES

... and respect to any women who get
THESE howlers on videotape!

She was begging for it.

Women adore me.

I can't help myself. I just love women so
much.

I can tell you want it.

I get headaches if I have to go more
than two days without it.

I was twelve.

That's never happened to me before.

I had to stop just to give her a rest.

At least twice a day.

Can't get enough of me.

Hundreds.

It's so big it's embarrassing.

Five hours.

It's not what you've got, it's how you use it.

CASANOVA? VAUXHALL NOVA, MORE LIKE...

What is it about men and sex? They drool over their ridiculous penismobiles, thinking their cars make them look like sex machines, but the sad truth is somewhat different...

'Men read maps better than women because only men can understand the concept of an inch equalling a hundred miles.'
ROSEANNE BARR, actor and comedian

'In this society, the norm of masculinity is phallic aggression. Male sexuality is, by definition, intensely and rigidly phallic. A man's identity is located in his conception of himself as the possessor of a phallus; a man's worth is located in his pride in phallic identity. The main characteristic of phallic identity is that worth is entirely contingent on the possession of a phallus. Since men have no other criteria for worth, no other notion of identity, those who do not have phalluses are not recognized as fully human.'

ANDREA DWORKIN,
feminist writer

'Most pitiful [are] the grown men who regard women as something to burnish their egos, a mere decoration for the end of their cock, the ones who had never learned to enjoy women's company.'

SANDY FAWKES, writer

'Men are those creatures with two legs and eight hands.'

JAYNE MANSFIELD, film star

'If men were as great lovers as they think they are, we women wouldn't have time to do our hair.'

MARLENE DIETRICH, actor and
singer

'Speaking of rapists, even the most die-hard feminist must admit that's one thing men do better than women.'

GABRIELLE BURTON, feminist writer

'Woman is: finally screwing and your groin and buttocks and thighs ache like hell and you're all wet and maybe bloody and it wasn't like a Hollywood movie at all but Jesus at least you're not a virgin any more but is this what it's all about? And meanwhile, he's asking, "Did you come?"'

ROBIN MORGAN, feminist writer and poet, *Sisterhood Is Powerful*

MEN'S LIES TO THEIR PARTNERS

But darling, you know I've been looking forward to it for weeks ...

You can't do it in this weather.

I'll handle this.

I *was* listening.

You know I could never look at someone else.

Of *course* I know what day this is.

I have to work late.

It wasn't expensive.

Do you think I enjoy travelling all over the world?

Men only, I'm afraid.

No, she wasn't there.

I'm just stopping off for a swift half.

I *am* within the speed limit.

You should've let me handle it.

I did it this morning.

I *don't* think you've put on weight.

Did I say I'd take care of it?

I didn't want to upset you.

There's plenty of time.

There's no reason for you to be jealous.

I have *not* been drinking.

It'll never happen again.

You wouldn't understand.

I remember exactly.

For heaven's sake, I was only kidding.

What policeman?

I don't snore.

Nothing's going to go wrong.

What woman?

I'm not taking sides.

Of course I like your mother.

I don't know how you can say a thing
like that to me.

It doesn't need a primer.

I only had one.

I love you.

I did follow your instructions.

I will *always* love you.

I'm happy if you're happy.

LOVE IS

... according to men!

'Many a man thinks yelling, "Is dinner ready?" is the same as saying "I love you."'

> MERLE SHAIN, writer

'The way to a man's heart is through his wife's belly, and don't you forget it.'

> EDWARD ALBEE, playwright,
> *Who's Afraid of Virginia Woolf?*

OH YEAH?

More lies, which they like to bring out when their partner isn't being co-operative, i.e. the man isn't getting his own way... diddums!

I thought *you* wanted to go OR I thought you *wanted* to go.

I'll make it up to you, I swear.

You're going to have a great time.

It's the last time I'll ask.

You don't have to do it if you don't want to.

Just a few of the chaps.

I distinctly remember that it was you who said it seemed like a great idea.

I'LL ALWAYS BE FAITHFUL TO YOU, HONEST

Hmm ...

I do.

This isn't the way it looks.

But, darling, you *know* you're the one I love.

She means *nothing* to me.

It was just that one time.

She's like a sister.

It was nothing.

We're just friends.

I thought you'd understand.

I'm not going to lie to you.

I am not.

I thought you knew.

I just couldn't help myself.

I'm sure I told you.

It's not what you think.

If you'll just let me explain …

I never meant for this to happen.

I was thinking of you the whole time.

I was drunk.

She's not my type.

She seduced *me*.

There's no reason for you to get so upset.

She wouldn't take 'no' for an answer.

I don't know how it happened.

I didn't enjoy it.

I don't even remember her name.

I WOULD TAKE YOU TO THE COMPANY'S CONFERENCE WEEKEND, BUT ...

And what do we think they get up to at conferences, eh? Sadly, we're probably right.

The kids need you at home.

No one else is taking his wife.

You wouldn't like it.

You think I'm going to be out enjoying myself, don't you? Well, I'm not. I'm going to be working my bollocks off the whole time.

*And after all those
lies, a truth:*

Why do so many women
fake orgasm?

*Because so many men
fake foreplay.*

DON'T WE JUST LOVE 'EM? WOMEN ON MEN

Here are some women after my own heart. They've certainly got men summed up.

'The more I see of men the more I admire dogs.'
MME DE SÉVIGNÉ, seventeenth-century
letter writer

'Men are nicotine-soaked, beer-besmirched, whiskey-greased, red-eyed devils.'
CARRY NATION, American temperance
campaigner

'A man ... is so in the way in the house!
ELIZABETH GASKELL,
writer, *Cranford*

'Whatever they may be in public life, whatever their relations with men, in their relations with women, all men are rapists, and that's all they are. They rape us with their eyes, their laws, and their codes.'

> MARILYN FRENCH, writer,
> *The Women's Room*

'Men build bridges and throw railroads across deserts, and yet they contend successfully that the job of sewing on a button is beyond them. Accordingly, they don't have to sew buttons.'

> HEYWOOD BROUN, writer,
> *Seeing Things at Night*

'Don't accept rides from strange men – and remember that all men are as strange as hell.'

> ROBIN MORGAN, feminist writer and
> poet, *Sisterhood Is Powerful*

'Women want mediocre men, and men are working hard to be as mediocre as possible.'

MARGARET MEAD, anthropologist

'Sometimes I wonder if men and women really suit each other. Perhaps they should live next door and just visit now and then.'

KATHARINE HEPBURN, actor

'What makes men so tedious
Is the need to show off and compete.
They'll bore you to death for hours and
hours before they'll admit defeat.'

WENDY COPE, poet, 'Men and their
boring arguments'

'The world men inhabit is rather bleak. It is a world full of doubt and confusion, where vulnerability must be hidden, not shared; where competition, not co-operation, is the order of the day; where men sacrifice the possibility of knowing their own children and sharing in their upbringing, for the sake of a job they may have chosen by chance, which may not suit them and which in many cases dominates their lives to the exclusion of much else.'

ANNA FORD, journalist and television newsreader

DON'T THEY JUST LOVE THEMSELVES? MEN ON MEN

Mind you, some men are sensitive enough to know that they're all quite stupid really. Here are some of them.

'Before a man speaks it is always safe to assume that he is a fool. After he speaks, it is seldom necessary to assume it.'

> H. L. MENCKEN, editor, essayist and philologist, *Sententiae*

'For most men life is a search for the proper manila envelope in which to get themselves filed.'

> CLIFTON FADIMAN, essayist

'Men cease to interest us when we find their limitations.'

> RALPH WALDO EMERSON, nineteenth-century essayist and poet

'I don't want to sound sexist here, but I think men do make better mall Santas: men have bigger bellies, men are used to sitting for long periods of time, and men have lots of experience making promises they have no intention of keeping.'

JAY LENO, American chat-show host

'Man is Nature's sole mistake!'

W. S. GILBERT, dramatist, humorist and librettist, *Princess Ida*

'A man's women folk, whatever their outward show of respect for his merit and authority, always regard him secretly as an ass and with something akin to pity . . . In this fact, perhaps, lies one of the best proofs of feminine intelligence or, as the common phrase makes it, feminine intuition.'

H. L. MENCKEN, editor, essayist and philologist, *In Defense of Women*

'Every man over forty is a scoundrel.'
GEORGE BERNARD SHAW, writer,
Man and Superman

'What passes for woman's intuition is often nothing more than man's transparency.'
GEORGE JEAN NATHAN, critic,
author and editor

'Men are the only animals that devote themselves, day in and day out, to making one another unhappy . . .'
H. L. MENCKEN, editor, essayist and
philologist, *Sententiae*

'I prefer rogues to imbeciles because they sometimes take a rest.'
ALEXANDRE DUMAS, *fils*,
nineteenth-century writer

WHAT ARE MEN LIKE?

Well, men are like lots of things:

Mascara
They usually run at the first sign of emotion.

•

Bike helmets
Handy in an emergency, but otherwise they just look silly.

•

Government bonds
They take so long to mature.

•

Parking spots
The good ones are taken, and the rest are too small.

•

Copiers
OK for reproduction, but that's about it.

•

Lava lamps
Fun to look at, but not all that bright.

•

Bank accounts
Without a lot of money, they don't
generate much interest.

•

High heels
They're easy to walk on once you get the
hang of it.

•

Curling irons
They're always hot, and they're always in
your hair.

•

Miniskirts
If you're not careful, they'll creep up
your legs.

•

Bananas
The longer you keep them the more limp
they go.

•

Place mats
They show up only when there's food on
the table.

•

Blenders
You need one, but you're not quite
sure why.

•

Commercials
You can't believe a word they say.

BEATING HIS CHEST...

Men at war

'War is the ultimate male ego trip.'
 BARBARA G. WALKER, feminist writer

'All men would be tyrants if they could.'
 ABIGAIL ADAMS,
 American letter writer

'Usually, when a lot of men get together,
it's called war.'
 MEL BROOKS, actor, comedian and
 film director

'If it's natural to kill, why do men have
to go into training to learn how?'
 JOAN BAEZ, folk singer

SHE SAYS ... HE SAYS ...

HER STORY

He was in an odd mood when I got to the bar; I thought it might have been because I was a bit late but he didn't say anything much about it. The conversation was quite slow going so I thought we should go off somewhere more intimate, where we could talk in private. We went to this restaurant, and he was *still* acting a bit funny, so I tried to cheer him up. I started to wonder whether it was me or something else, so I asked him, and he said 'No'. But, you know, I was not really sure.

Anyway, in the taxi back to his house I told him that I loved him but he just put his arm around me. I didn't know what the hell that meant because, you know, he didn't say it back or anything. We finally got back to his place and I feared he was going to dump me! I tried to ask him about it but he just switched on the TV. Somewhat depressed, I said, reluctantly, that I was tired and going to go to bed.

After about ten minutes, he joined me in bed and we had sex. Afterwards he still seemed really distracted, which made me just want to leave. I dunno, I just don't know what he thinks any more. I mean, do you think he's met someone else?

HIS STORY

Had a lousy day at work. Very tired. Got laid, though.

OK, GUYS, IT'S YOUR TURN

Yep. Gotta give the men a go – in the interests of balance, of course (and because my editor said I should). So the guys who helped me put this little book together came up with some really unpleasant things about being men. Don't bother getting your hankies out ...

We have to use men's toilets. At least women never have to go in the gents'.

We're blamed for everything! OK, so Adam took a bite from the forbidden fruit but you *know* Eve put him up to it.

We're expected to read the *Sun* or the bloody *Sport* and listen to *Radio Five Live*.

Have you tried to take a leak standing up when you've had one pint too many? (It was beer I spilled down 'em, honest.)

We're expected to remember footballers' names.

We don't have an excuse for laziness once every four weeks.

Everyone laughs at us if we can't open a jam jar.

We're expected to be some sort of use in a crisis, e.g. death of pet, flooded washing machine etc.

We're always expected to have in our pockets (a) cash, (b) keys, (c) spare keys (including car keys), (d) name and telephone number of 'that little place we went to with Fiona after Julia's wedding', (e) cash, (f) telephone number of 24-hour emergency locksmith/plumber/garage, (g) cash, (h) cash.

We have to put up, as good-naturedly as possible, with audacious comments from women which, if made of a woman by a man, would land the comment maker in serious trouble, e.g.: 'I suppose, [sneeringly] like all men, you fancy Anthea Turner/Posh Spice/Charlie Dimmock/Lady Thatcher/[insert female of choice].'

The embarrassment of jogger's willy.

We're expected to know the first thing about insurance/the Stock Market/ mortgages/ private health plans/ financial planning/bank codes of practice/ interest rates (now there's a misnomer)/the FTSE 100 etc.

We have to put on a brave face when confronted with muesli, quiche Lorraine, lentils, tahini, brown/wild rice, fennel-stick tea etc.

We get terminal flak for any resistance, however slight and however sensible, to suddenly mooted plans to move, redecorate, have babies etc.
Oh, and the thousand ills the (male) flesh is heir to, such as: socks (smelly); going bald; prostate cancer (kills more men per year in this country than breast cancer does women); hairs in the beak/ears and so on, and on...

The trials and tangulations of wearing boxer shorts.

Having to endure an hour and a half of supermarket shopping in the company of one's wife/mistress/girlfriend when you know that, by yourself, you could complete the entire shopping list (plus well-chosen alternatives for out-of-stock items) in 11 minutes 24 seconds (including queuing at till), thereby leaving one hour 18 minutes and 36 seconds for restorative in congenial bar/pub on the way home.

Being expected to be (a) good at DIY and (b) even remotely interested in it.

At a naturist resort, everyone notices when we have dirty thoughts.

We can't be in a position of power and be politically correct at the same time.

Finding out that one's wife's/mistress's/girlfriend's closest female friend hates and resents you with a passion bordering on the insane. For some reason this is an invariable rule – probably a tradition, or an old charter, or something.

A zip can be a health hazard.

We're hairy – and if we're not, people will make assumptions.

We learn hardly any new gossip at the hairdresser's.

Social conventions are extremely unfair to men. When a woman wants to prove that she's a real woman, all she needs to do is to have sex with a man. When, however, a man wants to prove that he's a real man, he needs to go through intensive training for several years to learn things like drinking beer to unconsciousness; pissing against the wind; spitting at least three metres ahead; and burping at 100dB. Once he is finally acknowledged into the 'Order of Real Men' and thus allowed to get off with a real woman, what is his reward? Nothing but steady complaints from his girlfriend whenever he practises his hard-earned skills.

OK, that's quite enough! (Poor loves! Doesn't your heart simply bleed for them, girls?)

RULES THAT MEN WISH WE GIRLS KNEW

All men have a number-one rule. Here are 30 of them:

1.

If *you* think you're fat, you probably are.

2.

Learn to work the toilet seat. If it's up, put it down. It will be up.

3.

If you ask a question you don't want an answer to, expect an answer you don't want to hear.

4.

Do not cut your hair. Ever. Long hair is always more attractive than short hair.

5.

Birthdays, Valentine's Day and anniversaries are *not* quests to find the perfect present or the largest bunch of flowers!

6.

I am *not* always thinking about you.
Live with it.

7.

Saturday=sports. It's like the full moon
or the changing of the tides. Let it be.

8.

Shopping is not a sport.

9.

When we have to go somewhere,
absolutely anything you wear is fine.

10.

You have *enough* clothes. You have *too
many* shoes.

11.

Crying is blackmail.

12.

Ex-boyfriends are idiots.

13.

Ask for what you want. Subtle hints do
not work.

14.

All anniversaries and social arrangements will be forgotten, even when we are reminded about them.

15.

'Yes' and 'no' are perfectly acceptable answers to most questions.

16.

Come to me with a problem only if you want help solving it. Sympathy is what your girlfriends are for.

17.

A headache that lasts for seventeen months is a problem. See a doctor.

18.

Foreign films are best left to foreigners.

19.

Anything we said six months ago is inadmissible in an argument.

20.
If something we said can be interpreted two ways, and one of the ways makes you sad or angry, we meant the other one.

21.
Don't rub the lamp if you don't want the genie to come out.

22.
If you know best how to do it, do it yourself.

23.
Say whatever you have to say during Fairy Liquid commercials.

24.
Women wearing Wonderbras and low-cut blouses lose their right to complain about having their boobs stared at.

25.
More women should wear Wonderbras and low-cut blouses.

26.

Our relationship is never going to be like it was during the first two months we were going out together. Get over it.

27.

Christopher Columbus did not need directions . . .

28.

If it itches, it will be scratched.

29.

If we ask what is wrong and you say 'nothing', we will act like nothing's wrong.

30.

Our lack of mind-reading ability is not proof of how little we care about you.

STRAIGHT WOMEN ON MEN

Men's idea of foreplay is taking their socks off.

It's only other people's husbands who cook.

They can't wait to tell you about their sexual conquests.

They drone on for hours about sport, when you know the only one they ALL take part in involves an armchair!
He agrees with me on one thing: I love him and he loves him.

Their idea of romance is to cuddle you from behind after coitus. I mean, who wants to feel a soft wet worm in the middle of their back? Yuckety, yuk, yuk!

They think they're so much better than
us at using computers.

When God created man, she was only
practising. Or it was a joke.

They've got such a range of emotions:
from A to B.

LESBIAN WOMEN ON MEN

They think we can't be satisfied without
their *thing* inside us!

They say things like, 'An hour with me
and she'll give up all this dyke
nonsense.'

They think women need men to have
and bring up kids. Wrong!

Their equipment reminds me of turkey
neck and turkey gizzard. Ugh!

STRAIGHT MEN ON MEN

They're always after my bird.

They always think they can do things better than I can, when I know it's the other way round.

They suddenly have an excuse to leave the bar when it's their turn to pay.

So many of them come from Essex.

Why can't they just *talk* into their mobile phones on trains?

GAY MEN ON MEN

Straight men are *hopeless* in bed.

Gay men are all the same: they're only ever on the lookout for the next lay.

Straight men hate poofs. (Hey! I'm allowed to use that word – you're not, OK?)

Gay men think the Board of Trade is a bench in Hyde Park.

It takes six gay men to change a sodding light bulb: two to go to Ikea to choose it, one to screw it in and three more to come round and admire it over drinks.

ELEMENTAL, MY DEAR . . .

Two new additions to the periodic table of elements:

Element Name: WOMAN

Symbol: WO

Atomic Weight: (don't even go there)

Physical Properties: Generally round in form. Boils at nothing and may freeze at any time. Melts whenever treated properly. Very bitter if mishandled.

Chemical Properties: Very active. Highly unstable. Possesses strong affinity with gold, silver, platinum, and precious stones. Volatile when left alone. Able to absorb great amounts of exotic food. Turns slightly green when placed next to a shinier specimen.

Usage: Highly ornamental. An extremely good catalyst for dispersion of wealth. Probably the most powerful income-reducing agent known.

Caution: Highly explosive in inexperienced hands.

•

Element Name: MAN

Symbol: XY

Atomic Weight: (200+/-100)

Physical Properties: Solid at room temperature, but gets bent out of shape easily. Fairly dense and sometimes flaky. Difficult to find a pure sample. Due to rust, ageing samples are unable to conduct electricity as easily as young samples.

Chemical Properties: Attempts to bond with WO any chance it can get. Also tends to form strong bonds with itself. Becomes explosive when mixed with KD (Element: Child) for prolonged period of time. Neutralize by saturating with alcohol.

Usage: None known. Possibly good methane source. Good specimens are able to produce large quantities on command.

Caution: In the absence of WO, this element rapidly decomposes and begins to smell.

THE ULTIMATE GUY QUIZ:

1. In the company of females, intercourse should be referred to as:

    a) lovemaking
    b) screwing
    c) the pigskin bus pulling into
       tuna town

2. You should make love to a woman for the first time only after you've both shared:

    a) your views about what you expect
       from a sexual relationship
    b) your blood-test results
    c) five tequila slammers

3. You time your orgasm so that:

    a) your partner climaxes first
    b) you both climax simultaneously
    c) you don't miss *Match of the Day*

4. Passionate, spontaneous sex on the kitchen floor is:

    a) healthy, creative love-play
    b) not the sort of thing your
       wife/girlfriend would ever agree to
    c) not the sort of thing your
       wife/girlfriend need ever find
       out about

5. Spending the whole night cuddling a woman you've just had sex with is:

    a) the best part of the experience
    b) the second best part of the
       experience
    c) £100 extra

6. Your girlfriend says she's gained five pounds in weight in the last month. You tell her that it is:

    a) no concern of yours
    b) not a problem, she can join your gym
    c) a conservative estimate

7. You think today's sensitive, caring man is:

    a) a myth
    b) an oxymoron
    c) a moron

8. Foreplay is to sex as:

    a) appetizer is to entree
    b) primer is to paint
    c) a queue is to an amusement
       park ride

9. Which of the following are you most likely to find yourself saying at the end of a relationship?

    a) "I hope we can still be friends."
    b) "I'm not in right now, please leave
       a message at the beep."
    c) "Welcome to Dumpsville,
population, YOU."

10. A woman who is uncomfortable watching you masturbate:
- a) probably needs more time before she can cope with that sort of intimacy
- b) is uptight and a waste of time
- c) shouldn't have sat next to you on the bus in the first place

If you answered "a" more than 7 times, check your pants to make sure you really are a man.

If you answered "b" more than seven times, check into therapy, you're still a little confused.

If you answered "c" more then 7 times.............YOU DA MAN!!!!!

50 REASONS IT'S GREAT TO BE A BLOKE

1.

You never get pissed as fast as the chick you're hitting on.

2.

If you wear a suit and tie no one will think you're a lesbian.

3.

You have no trouble whatsoever putting stuff off until tomorrow.

4.

You get to operate heavy machinery.

5.

You don't collapse in floods of tears if your partner says you look fine.

6.

You feel perfectly comfortable wearing clothes you wore yesterday and left on the floor all night.

7.

You're allowed to (even expected to) sweat heavily.

8.

You can eat a banana while walking past a building site.

9.

Telephone conversations are over in 30 seconds, no problem.

10.

Push-ups are a lot easier.

11.

The remote is yours and yours alone.

12.

You're applauded by your mates for farting in public.

13.

You can buy condoms without the pharmacist imagining you naked.

14.

You don't have to leave the room to make an emergency tackle rearrangement.

15.

People never glance at your tits when you're talking to them.

16.

Hot wax never comes near your genitals.

17.

Ricky Martin doesn't live in your universe.

18.

You can whip your shirt off on a hot day.

19.

Cricket seems like a good idea.

20.

You don't have to curl up next to a hairy arse every night.

21.

Nobody secretly wonders if you swallow.

22.

You can piss standing up.

23.

Stag parties shit all over hen nights.

24.

Not liking a person does not preclude
having an enjoyable sh*g with them.

25.

The world is your urinal.

26.

Your bathroom queues are
80% shorter.

27.

Guys in hockey masks don't
attack you.

28.

When flicking through the TV channels,
you don't have to stop on every shot of
someone crying.

29.
You can open all your own jars.

30.
Same work, more pay.

31.
You can turn the bath into a
beauty spa.

32.
You can go years without having to see a
doctor.

33.
If you own a toaster you're never more
than 2 minutes away from a tasty meal.

34.
Your arse is never a factor in a job
interview.

35.
A 5-day holiday requires only
1 suitcase.

36.

You know at least 20 ways to open a beer bottle.

37.

Your undies are under £5 for a pack of three.

38.

If another bloke shows up to a party in the same outfit, you might become lifelong mates.

39.

As long as your mum's still alive, you can get your washing done at her place.

40.

Wedding dress £1,000; suit rental £50.

41.

You can have as many sexual partners as you like and get called a stud.

42.

Porn movies are designed with your mind in mind.

43.

Haircuts cost £5.

44.

You can get a blow job.

45.

You can become a Catholic priest and have unlimited access to free wine.

46.

You understand the offside rule.

47.

None of your co-workers have the power to make you cry.

48.

If you don't call a mate when you say you will, he won't tell all your other mates you've changed.

49.

You know stuff about tanks.

50.

You think the idea of drop-kicking a small dog is funny.

JOKES (AT MEN'S EXPENSE)

What's the difference between a man and a catfish?

One's a bottom-feeding scum-sucker and the other is a fish.

•

What did the experts of the nineties discover that could do the work of ten men?

One woman.

•

What's the difference between whales and men?

Whales mate for life.

•

How are men like commercials?

You can't believe a word either one says and they both last about sixty seconds.

•

What do men and beer bottles have in common?

They're both empty from the neck up.

•

Why are men like laxatives?

They both irritate the sh*t out of you.

•

How are men like the weather?

Nothing can be done to change either of them.

•

What do men and decaffeinated coffee have in common?

No active ingredients.

●

How many men does it take to screw in a lightbulb?

Just one. They'll screw anything.

●

How many men does it take to change a lightbulb?

Ten, one to change the lightbulb, and nine to congratulate him down the pub.

●

What is a man's idea of commitment?

A second date.

●

Why do men name their penises?

Because they want to be on a first name basis with the person who makes 95 per cent of their decisions.

•

Why were men given larger brains than dogs?

So they they wouldn't hump women's legs at cocktail parties.

•

What is a man's idea of foreplay?

Half an hour of begging.

•

What does a man think foreplay is?

Something you do on a golf course.

•

How did the man save a woman from being attacked?

He controlled himself.

•

What does a man say when he finds his wife in bed with her lover?

What are you doing?

•

What's the difference between a man and a yeti?

One is covered with matted hair and stinks. The other lives on the top of a mountain.

•

What's the difference between a man
and a yoghurt?

Yoghurt has culture.

•

What does a man say before he picks his
nose?

Grace.

•

What's the difference between a man
and a monkey?

*A monkey can be trained to take out
the garbage.*

•

Why is a man like Santa Claus?

Because he only comes once a year.

•

What's the best way to get a man to remember your anniversary?

Get married on his birthday.

•

How does a man help with the housework?

He lifts his leg as you vacuum.

•

What do men and dog poo have in commmon?

The older they get the easier they are to pick up.

•

Why do men act stupid?

Who says they're acting?

•

What's the difference between a stupid man and an intelligent man?

Nothing, they both think that they know everything.

•

Why doesn't a man believe in the new Messiah?

Because to him a second coming is an impossibility.

•

Did you hear about the man who makes love like he drives his car?

He goes too fast and gets there before anyone else.

•

What do you call a man who tidies up
after himself?

An over-achiever.

•

What's the best way to keep a man
happy in the bedroom?

*Put the TV in the bedroom and turn on
the football.*

•

How do you keep a man from wanting
sex?

Marry him.

•

How do you keep a man from wanting
the other woman?

Divorce him.

•

What does a man do when confronted with a toddler having a tantrum?

Stamps his feet and shouts for mother.

•

What do you call a man who uses the rhythm method?

Dad.

•

Why did the man throw away his toilet brush?

He discovered toilet paper.

•

What's a man's idea of a varied diet?

A quarter-pounder with cheese one day, and without cheese the next.

•

Why don't men's dogs do tricks?

You have to be more intelligent than a dog to teach it tricks.

•

What's the difference between a man and a vibrator?

A vibrator can't mow the lawn.

•

How can you tell if a man is cheating on you?

He has a bath more than once a month.

•

What's a man's idea of safe sex?

Masturbation.

•

What quality do most men look for in a woman?

Breathing.

•

How does a man make sex more interesting?

He leaves town.

•

How did the wife stop her husband biting his nails?

She made him wear shoes.

•

What's the useless piece of skin attached to the male member.

A man.

•

What does a man say when he proposes
marriage?

You're going to have a what?

•

Why did the man put his willy in boiling
water?

His wife told him to get sterilised.

•

There was a man so stupid he didn't
know arson from incest.

He set fire to his sister.

•

How are men like dogs?

*One stroke and they follow you
everywhere.*

•

How many men does it take to change the toilet roll?

Don't know, its never happened before.

Why does a man like having two women in bed?

I: So that he can come and go at the same time.

II: So that he can see double without having to buy a drink.

III: So that they have someone to talk to.

What is a man's idea of safe sex?

I: Not doing it on top of scaffolding.

II: Doing it when his wife's away.

III: Giving you a false name and address.

•

A man's idea of a balanced diet is:

I: Eating on one leg.

II: Leaving the crusts on his egg soldiers.

III: A six-pack in each hand.

Why do men think that masturbation is better than intercourse?

I: Because they don't have to buy flowers.

II: Because they don't have to make conversation.

III: Because they don't have to look their best.

How are men like Chinese meals?

They satisfy you, but only for a little while.

●

What's a man's idea of foreplay?

'You awake?'

•

Why do men enjoy fishing so much?

Because it's the only time anyone says to them 'Wow! That's a big one!'

•

How are men and spray paint alike?

One squeeze and they're all over you.

•

Why do men like being legless?

It's the only time they can boast that their willies touch the floor.

•

What's the difference between a man and a condom?

Condoms are no longer thick and insensitive.

●

Why don't men suffer from haemorrhoids?

Because they're such perfect arseholes.

●

How do you know when a man's had an orgasm?

He snores.

●

How is a man like a set of car keys?

Both are easily mislaid.

●

How is a man like the local council complaints office?

Both are impossible to get through to when you need to talk.

•

What's a man's idea of fairness in a relationship?

Once with a condom on, once without.

•

What does a man think of circumcision?

It's a rip off.

•

Why do men talk about football?

Because it would be boring to talk about tits all the time.

•

What's a man's idea of DIY?

Making a cling-film condom.

●

What do you get when you have two little balls in your hand?

Your man's undivided attention.

●

What's the difference between a man and a good book?

You get pleasure out of a good book.

●

What's the difference between a man and wine?

Wine matures.

●

Why do men become smarter during sex?

Because they're plugged into a genius.

•

Why don't women have men's brains?

Because they don't have penises to put them in.

•

Why did God make man before woman?

She needed a rough draft before she made the final copy.

•

Why is a man's pee yellow and his sperm white?

So he can tell if he's coming or going.

•

How can you tell if a man is sexually excited?

He's breathing.

•

How do you scare off a man?

Tell him you love him and you want his children.

•

Why do gentlemen prefer blondes?

They like people of their own intellectual ability.

•

What do you call a man with an IQ of 50?

Gifted.

•

How do men sort out their laundry?

Filthy, and filthy but wearable.

•

What's the diffference between a man
and ET?

ET phoned home.

•

Why is a psychoanalysis quicker for
men than for women?

*Because when it's time to go back to their
childhood, they're already there.*

•

How many men does it take to tile a
bathroom?

It depends how thinly you slice them.

•

Why do men's hearts make the best transplants?

They've never been used.

•

Why are men like chocolates?

They never last long enough.

•

How do men exercise on the beach?

They suck in their stomachs when they see a bikini.

•

Why is it dangerous to let a man's mind wander?

It's too little to be allowed out on its own.

•

What do you do if your best friend runs
off with your husband?

You miss her dreadfully.

•

What's the difference between a man
and giving birth?

*One is painful, almost unbearable,
whilst the other is just having a baby.*

•

What do you call a man wearing
handcuffs?

Trustworthy.

SOME (FAMOUS) WOMEN ARE BITCHES

Dorothy Parker:
I require only three things of a man. He must be handsome, ruthless and stupid.

•

Rita Rudner:
I was a ballerina. I had to quit after I injured a groin muscle. It wasn't mine.

•

Lynn Hecht Schafren:
Why is it that men can be bastards and women must wear pearls and smile?

•

Rhonda Dickison:
If you love someone, set them free. If they come back, they're probably broke.

Angela Matin:

Q: What do you do when your boyfriend walks out?

A: Shut the door.

•

Jay Behar:

I'm at a point where I want a man in my house! Just come in, attach the VCR, and get out.

•

Roseanne:

A guy is a lump like a doughnut. So, first you gotta get rid of all the stuff his mum did to him, and then you gotta get rid of all that macho crap that they pick up from the beer commercials. And then there's my personal favourite, the male ego.

•

Cynthia Heimel:

A woman needs a man like a fish needs
a net.

•

Mamie Van Doren:

(on Warren Beatty) He's the type of man
who will end up dying in his own arms.

•

Bette Davis:

The male ego with few exceptions is
elephantine to start with.

•

Nancy Astor:

In passing, also, I would like to say that
the first time Adam had a chance he
laid the blame on woman.

•

Roseanne:

Men can read maps better than women.
'Cause only the male mind could
conceive of one inch equalling a hundred
miles.

•

Donna Gephart:

If brevity is the soul of wit, your penis
must be a riot.

•

Judy Tenuta:

How many of you ever started dating
someone because you were too lazy to
commit suicide?

•

Erika Ritter:

I believe in women. Men are just
unsubstantiated rumours.

•

Coco Chanel:
As long as you know that most men are like children you know everything.

•

Raquel Welch:
There aren't any hard women, only soft men.

•

Margaret Mead:
Women want mediocre men, and men are working hard to become as mediocre as possible.

•

Ruth Gordon:
In our family we don't divorce our men — we bury them.

•

Gloria Steinem:
(If men could menstruate) sanitary supplies would be federally funded and free. Of course, some men would still pay for the prestige of such commercial brands as Paul Newman Tampons, Muhammed Ali's Rope-a-Dope Pads, John Wayne Maxi Pads, and Joe Namath Jock Shields – 'For Those Light Bachelor Days'.

•

Roseanne:
If men really knew how to do it, they wouldn't have to pay for it.

•

Cher:
The trouble with some women is that they get all excited about nothing – and then marry him.

•

Jessica Tandy:
When he's late for dinner, I know he's either having an affair or is lying dead in the street. I always hope it's the street.

•

Elaine Boosler:
My ancestors wandered lost in the wilderness for forty years because, even in biblical times, men would not stop to ask for directions.

•

Anon:
If they can put a man on the moon . . . why can't they put them all there?

•

Madonna:
I wouldn't want a penis. It would be like
a third leg. It would seem like a
contraption that would get in your way.

•

Camille Paglia:
There is no female Mozart because there
is no female Jack the Ripper.

•

Katherine Anne Porter:
It's a man's world,
and you men
can have it.

•

EPILOGUE

I hope you've enjoyed my little bitchathon.

I've got simply *oodles* more little stories and titbits about men – so many that you'd need a computer disk the size of a man's ego to store them. So I may be back again. If you have any thoughts to share, do write or e-mail me c/o my publisher: **jokes@michaelomarabooks.com** We always welcome new contributions, but regret that space does not allow for individual credits.

Toodle-oo darlings!

All Michael O'Mara titles are available by post from:

Bookpost, P.O. Box 29, Douglas, Isle of Man IM99 1BQ

Credit cards accepted. Please telephone 01624 836000
Fax 01624 837033
Internet http://www.bookpost.co.uk

Free postage and packing in the UK.
Overseas customers allow £1 per book (paperbacks)
and £3 per book (hardbacks)

Other humour titles:

The World's Stupidest Laws – ISBN 1-85479-549-X
The World's Stupidest Signs – ISBN 1-85479-555-4
Outrageous Expressions – ISBN 1-85479-556-2
Totally Stupid Men – ISBN 1-85479-274-1
Stupid Men Quiz Book – ISBN 1-85479-693-3
Complete Crap – ISBN 1-85479-313-6
Wicked Cockney Rhyming Slang – ISBN 1-85479-386-1
The Ultimate Book of Farting – ISBN 1-85479-596-1
The Complete Book of Farting – ISBN 1-85479-440-X
The History of Farting – ISBN 1-85479-754-9
Veni Vidi Vici: Over 450 Laughable Latin Phrases – ISBN 1-85479-441-8
Going to Hades is Easy – ISBN 1-85479-589-9
Witty, Wicked & Wise – ISBN 1-85479-593-7
The Ultimate Insult – ISBN 1-85479-288-1
The Little Englander's Handbook – ISBN 1-85479-553-8